This Christmas Coloring Book

Belongs To:

____

____

Date: ____/____/____

Write and Draw to Express Yourself

Date: ____/____/____

Date: ___ / ___ / ___

Write and Draw to Express Yourself

Date: ___/___/___

Date: ____/____/____

Write and Draw to Express Yourself

Date: ____/____/____

Date: ____/____/____

Write and Draw to Express Yourself

Date: ____/____/____

Date: ____/____/____

Write and Draw to Express Yourself

Date: ___/___/___

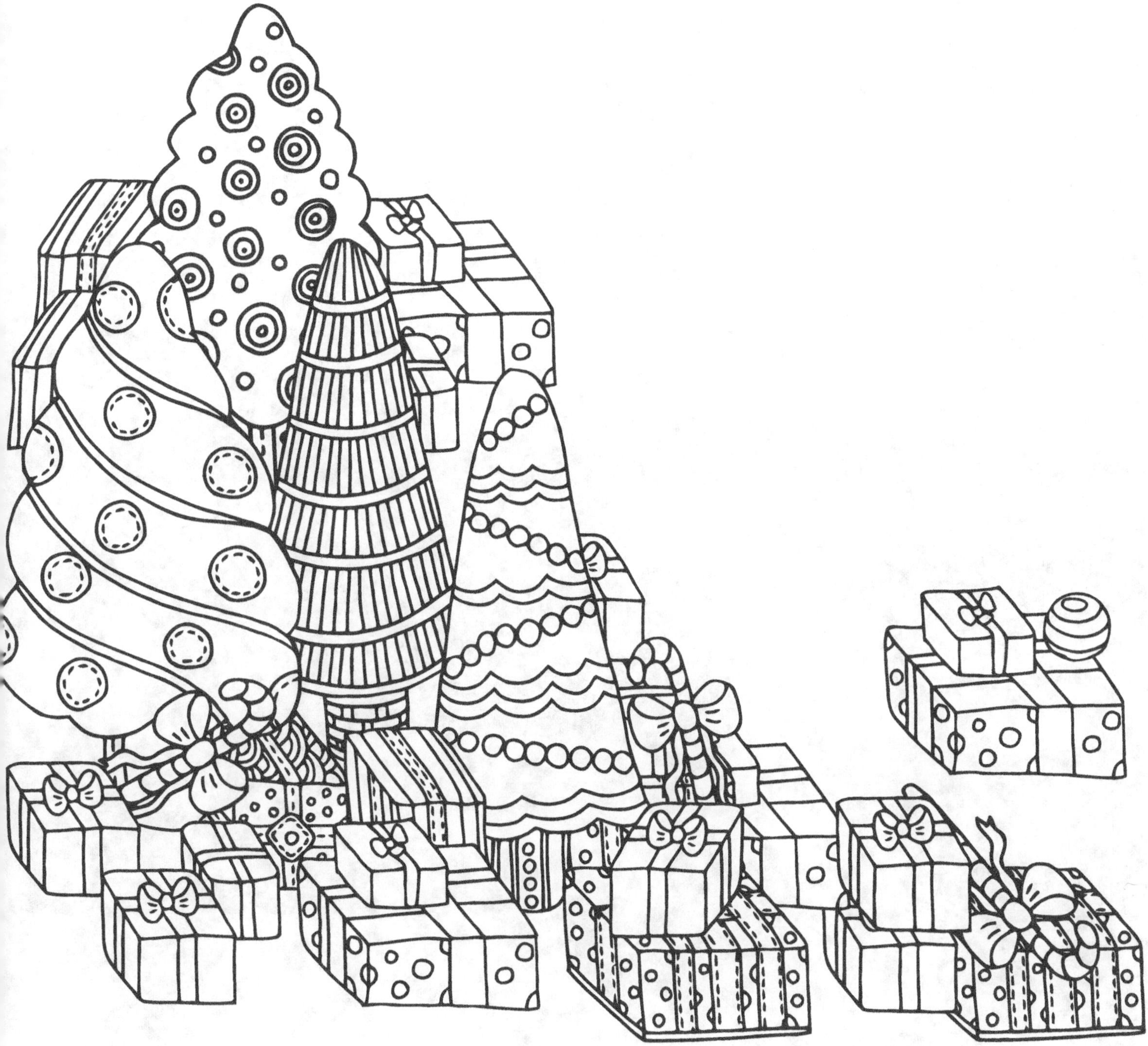

Date: ___/___/___

Write and Draw to Express Yourself

Date: ____/____/____

Date: ___/___/___

Write and Draw to Express Yourself

Date: ____/____/____

Date: ____ / ____ / ____

Write and Draw to Express Yourself

Date: ____/____/____

Date: ____/____/____

Write and Draw to Express Yourself

Date: ___ / ___ / ___

Date: ____/____/____

Write and Draw to Express Yourself

Date: ___/___/___

Date: _____/_____/_____

Write and Draw to Express Yourself

Date: ___/___/___

Date: ___/___/___

Write and Draw to Express Yourself

Date: ___/___/___

Date: ____/____/____

Write and Draw to Express Yourself

Date: ___/___/___

Write and Draw to Express Yourself

Date: ____/____/____

Date: ____/____/____

Write and Draw to Express Yourself

Date: ____/____/____

Date: ____/____/____

Write and Draw to Express Yourself

Date: ___/___/___

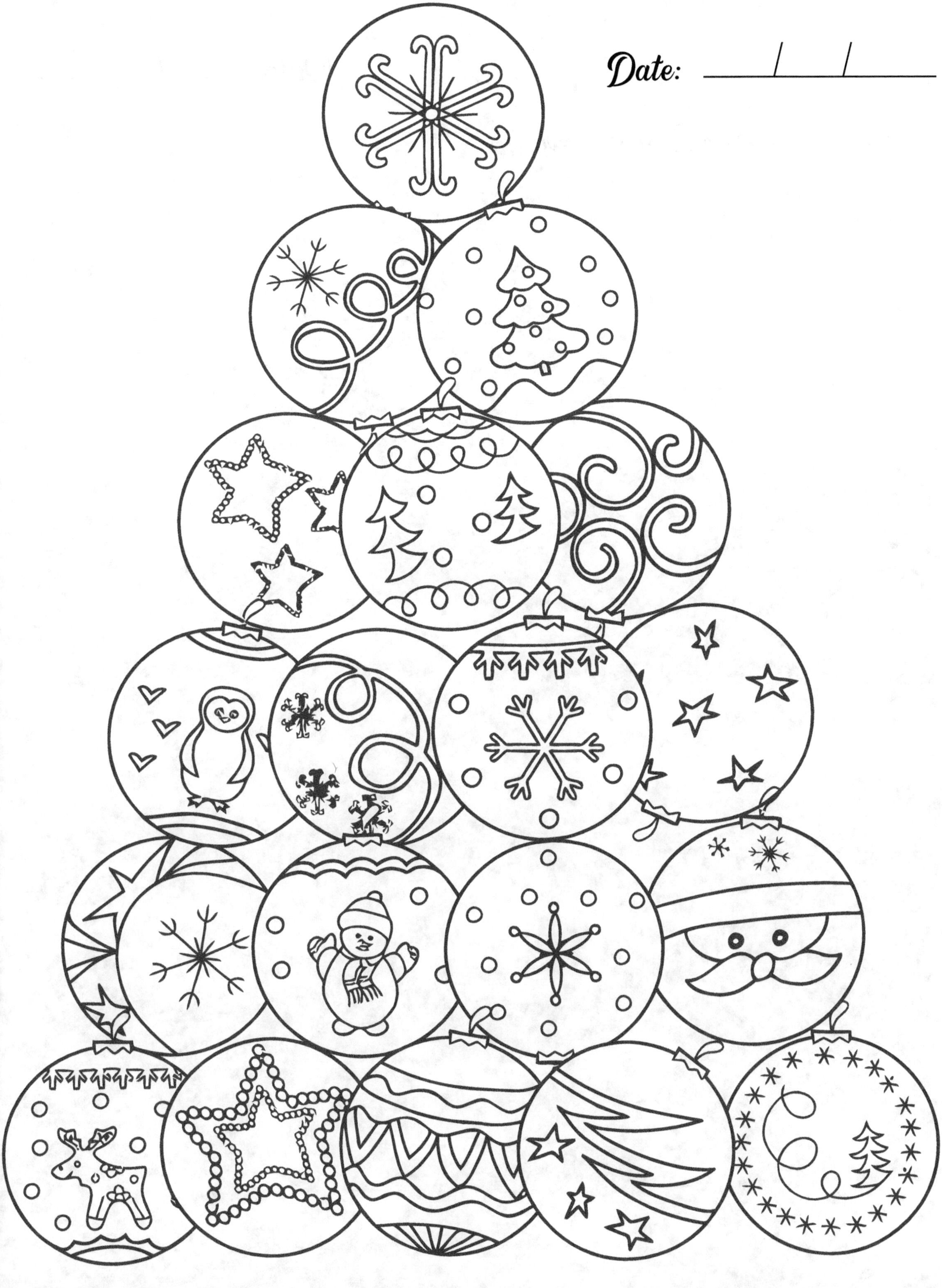

Date: _____ / _____ / _____

Write and Draw to Express Yourself

Date: ____/____/____

Date: ___/___/___

Write and Draw to Express Yourself

Date: ____/____/____

Date: ___/___/___

Write and Draw to Express Yourself

Date: ___/___/___

Date: _____/_____/_____

Write and Draw to Express Yourself

Date: ____/____/____

Date: ___/___/___

Write and Draw to Express Yourself

Date: ____/____/____

Date: ____/____/____

Write and Draw to Express Yourself

Date: ___/___/___

Write and Draw to Express Yourself

Date: ____/____/____

Date: ___/___/___

Write and Draw to Express Yourself

The Magic of Christmas

Date: ____/____/____

Write and Draw to Express Yourself

Date: ____/____/________

Write and Draw to Express Yourself

Date: ____/____/____

Date: _____ / _____ / _____

Write and Draw to Express Yourself

Date: ___/___/___

Write and Draw to Express Yourself

Date: ___/___/___

Write and Draw to Express Yourself

Date: ___/___/___

Date: ____/____/____

Write and Draw to Express Yourself

Date: ____/____/____

Date: ___/___/___

Write and Draw to Express Yourself

Date: ___/___/___

Date: ___/___/___

Write and Draw to Express Yourself

Date: ___/___/___

Write and Draw to Express Yourself

Date: ____ / ____ / ____

Write and Draw to Express Yourself

peace
&
joy

Date: ___ / ___ / ___

Write and Draw to Express Yourself

Date: ____/____/____

Date: ____/____/____

Write and Draw to Express Yourself

Date: ___/___/___

Date: ___/___/___

Write and Draw to Express Yourself

Date: ____/____/________

Date: ____/____/____

Write and Draw to Express Yourself

Date: ____/____/____

Write and Draw to Express Yourself

Date: ___/___/___

Date: ____/____/____

Write and Draw to Express Yourself

Date: ____/____/____

Date: _____/_____/_____

Write and Draw to Express Yourself

Date: ____/____/________

Date: ____/____/____

Write and Draw to Express Yourself

Date: ____/____/____

www.ingramcontent.com/pod-product-compliance
Lightning Source LLC
Chambersburg PA
CBHW081532220526
45467CB00010B/3155
* 9 7 8 1 7 0 8 1 4 2 8 9 6 *